CLASSICAL SOLOS
FOR
CLARINET

15 Easy Solos for Contest and Performance
Arranged by Philip Sparke

ONLINE MEDIA INCLUDED
Audio Recordings
Printable Piano Accompaniments

PLAYBACK+
Speed • Pitch • Balance • Loop

To access recordings and PDF accompaniments visit:
www.halleonard.com/mylibrary

Enter Code
5479-8401-3336-7320

ISBN 978-1-70516-739-7

Visit Hal Leonard Online at
www.halleonard.com

World headquarters, contact:
Hal Leonard
7777 West Bluemound Road
Milwaukee, WI 53213
Email: info@halleonard.com

In Europe, contact:
Hal Leonard Europe Limited
1 Red Place
London, W1K 6PL
Email: info@halleonardeurope.com

In Australia, contact:
Hal Leonard Australia Pty. Ltd.
4 Lentara Court
Cheltenham, Victoria, 3192 Australia
Email: info@halleonard.com.au

WALTZ

B♭ CLARINET

MORITZ VOGEL
Arranged by PHILIP SPARKE

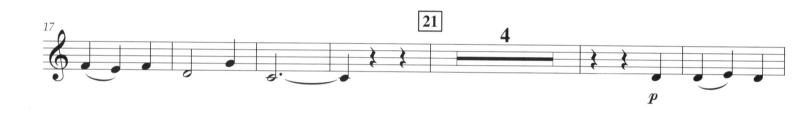

00870092

CHORALE

Now praise, my soul, the Lord

JOHANN SEBASTIAN BACH
Arranged by PHILIP SPARKE

B♭ CLARINET

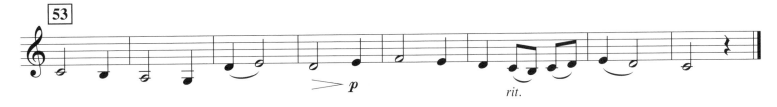

00870092

HUMMING SONG

from *Album for the Young*

Bb CLARINET

ROBERT SCHUMANN
Arranged by PHILIP SPARKE

Moderato (♩ = 94)

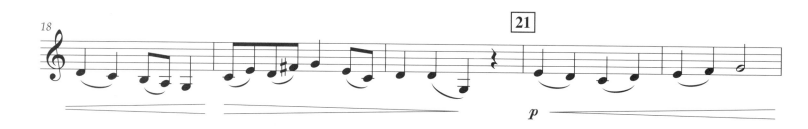

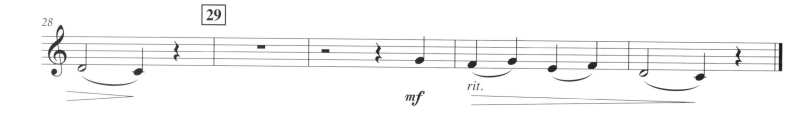

GYMNOPÉDIE NO. 1

ERIK SATIE
Arranged by PHILIP SPARKE

B♭ CLARINET

00870092

I'M CALLED LITTLE BUTTERCUP

from *HMS Pinafore*

Bb CLARINET

SIR ARTHUR SULLIVAN
Arranged by PHILIP SPARKE

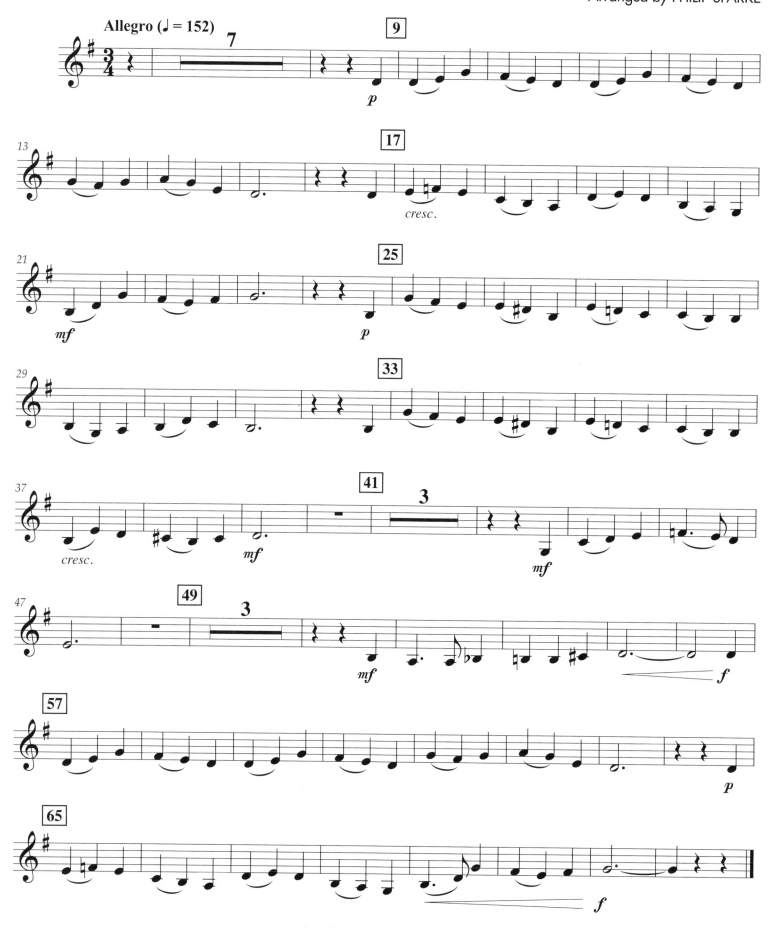

STUDY
Op. 37, No. 3

HENRY LEMOINE
Arranged by PHILIP SPARKE

B♭ CLARINET

00870092

MINUET
(Z. 649)

Bb CLARINET

HENRY PURCELL
Arranged by PHILIP SPARKE

THEME AND VARIATION

from *Sonatina No. 3*

THOMAS ATTWOOD
Arranged by PHILIP SPARKE

Bb CLARINET

NORTHERN SONG

from *Album for the Young*

B♭ CLARINET

ROBERT SCHUMANN
Arranged by PHILIP SPARKE

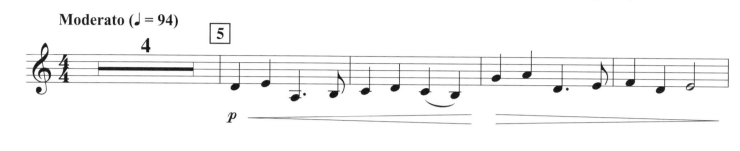

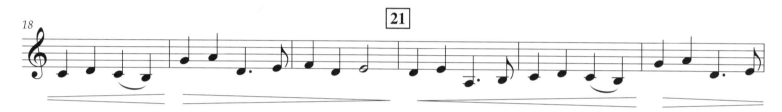

TWO GERMAN DANCES

from *Twelve German Dances, D. 420*

FRANZ SCHUBERT
Arranged by PHILIP SPARKE

Bb CLARINET

00870092

WATCHMAN'S SONG

from *Lyric Pieces, Op. 12*

B♭ CLARINET

EDVARD GRIEG
Arranged by PHILIP SPARKE

GAVOTTE

B♭ CLARINET

JAN LADISLAV DUSSEK
Arranged by PHILIP SPARKE

VIEN QUÀ, DORINA BELLA

Bb CLARINET

ANTONIO BIANCHI
Transcribed by **C. M. von WEBER**
Arranged by PHILIP SPARKE

MINUET

from *Notebook for Anna Magdalena Bach*

B♭ CLARINET

Attributed to **CHRISTIAN PETZOLD**
Arranged by PHILIP SPARKE

00870092

THE PRINCE OF DENMARK'S MARCH

from *Choice Lessons for the Harpsichord or Spinet*

Bb CLARINET

JEREMIAH CLARKE
Arranged by PHILIP SPARKE